Orkney in Photographs 2

Published by The Orcadian (Kirkwall Press)
Hell's Half Acre, Kirkwall, Orkney, KW15 1GJ
Tel: 01856 879000 Fax: 01856 879001
www.orcadian.co.uk
Book sales: www.orcadian.co.uk/shop/index.php
Photograph sales: www.theorcadianphotos.co.uk

Pictures: Tom O'Brien Words: James Miller

ISBN No: 978-1-902957-54-8

Printed by The Orcadian, Hatston Print Centre,
Hell's Half Acre, Kirkwall, Orkney, Scotland, KW15 1GJ

Tom O'Brien is the staff photographer at *The Orcadian*, the weekly newspaper in Orkney.

He was born in Glasgow and lived most of his early life in Livingston, before moving to Orkney in 2005 to be closer to his wife's extended family.

He became interested in photography at an early age and was processing black and white films when he was only eight years old. Tom was 13 when his first picture was published; a sports picture in the *West Lothian Courier*.

He has had a variety of jobs during his adult life, but photography has always been his passion. He worked as a photographer for the Territorial Army and three police forces.

Tom and his wife, Diane, have two of a family.

Vat of Kirbister, Stronsay. This is a natural arch on the east coast of the island of Stronsay. It can be a dramatic place in winter, when fierce storms whip up a swell that crashes under the "bridge". The Vat and surrounding picturesque coastline is easily accessible for walkers, and can be incorporated in a round stroll of various lengths.

Cruise liners. These vessels calling in at Orkney are a very common summer sight and a relatively recent development. Tourism is a vital part of the local economy, and the cruise-liner trade is a key and growing component.

Most of the famous names have called, including Cunard's *Queen Elizabeth*. The "season" is from spring through to autumn – none venture here in winter! – and liners normally arrive overnight, anchor in Kirkwall Bay and ferry their passengers ashore in lifeboats and tenders, probably to avoid berthing charges in many cases. However, it is anticipated that a recently constructed deep-water quay at Hatston (principally for renewables industry vessels) will also be utilised by the cruise liners.

Passengers spend a full day on the Mainland, visiting the historic sites and shopping. Many prefer to avoid the organised coach tour and hire private vehicles, escorted and otherwise, to see Orkney at their leisure.

The liner pictured is the *Crown Princess*, and to the rear is one of the North Isles internal ferries returning to Kirkwall.

CROWN PRINCESS
HAMILTON

Island ferry services. The "outer" islands of Orkney are serviced by a fleet of ferries run by the local authority through a company called, unsurprisingly Orkney Ferries. The islands council operates a subsidised service with a fleet of nine vessels, varying in size from a small passenger-only boat (between Westray and Papa Westray) to the vessels pictured. The latter ply between Kirkwall and the larger North Isles; two are named after Norse earls, *Sigurd* and *Thorfinn*, and the one pictured in the foreground is the *Varagen.*

She was originally bought by Orkney Islands Council in the 1980s as part of a controversial and costly plan to start a "short sea route" service across the Pentland Firth from Burwick, in South Ronaldsay, but it ended in disaster and the vessel was reassigned to her present role.

Replacement of the larger vessels to more modern standards is currently under consideration.

The isles service is excellent, with daily return trips possible to nearly all the islands. Some people living on islands close to the Mainland, such as Rousay, Shapinsay, Flotta and Hoy, "commute" to work by ferry.

VARAGEN

Wartime aviation. In recent years there has been an upsurge of interest in the world wars and the strategic role Orkney played in these conflicts.

Orkney, in wartime, was principally known as a naval base, but in fact there were four separate aerodromes here in the Second World War – two in the West Mainland, one at Hatston (now the industrial estate on the outskirts of Kirkwall) and Grimsetter, the present civil airport.

Local wartime interest has led to the formation of a group called ARGOS (Aviation Research Group Orkney and Shetland) that is dedicated to recording all aspects of aviation history around the Northern Isles.

Our picture shows them excavating the site of a crashed Spitfire that was involved in a mid-air collision in 1943. The other aircraft, also a Spitfire, ditched in the sea, but this one crashed in the parish of Rendall. Sadly, the 23-year-old pilot, who was based at HMS *Sparrowhawk* (Hatston), perished, and is buried in St Olaf Cemetery, outside Kirkwall.

ARGOS has a very good website, http://www.crashsiteorkney.com/

A.R.G.O.S.

BROUGH OF BIRSAY

ST MAGNUS CATHEDRAL

The Scottish Primrose, *Primula scotica*, or the Flower of Scotland. Whatever name you choose to call this charming little flower, sadly you will not find it nationally, despite its name. In fact, you will only spot it in Orkney, Caithness and Sutherland.

There are permanent fears over the future of this rare plant, and regular surveys sometimes suggest that it is disappearing fast in some areas. It grows mainly in short grassland close to the sea, often near the top of cliffs.

In Orkney, people should be on the lookout around May to July, and common sites are at Yesnaby, the west coasts of Rousay and Westray, Papay (Papa Westray), North Hill and South Walls.

It is very distinctive, and has a flower around eight millimetres in diameter with five heart-shaped petals and a bright yellow centre.

An officer from Scottish Natural Heritage was once quoted as saying: "*Primula scotica* is best appreciated with one's face close to the ground so that you can achieve an excellent view of the flower with its pink petals and yellow centre."

Whether you wish to view it in this posture is up to personal choice, but they must NOT be picked under any circumstances.

ONE POUND

Maeshowe. There are chambered cairns all over Orkney, but the biggest and best-known is Maeshowe, in the parish of Stenness, alongside the main Kirkwall – Stromness road.

The cairn is precisely positioned so that the setting sun at the winter solstice (and for several weeks at that time) shines directly down the long entrance passage and on to the back wall of the tomb – a kind of Indiana Jones moment for those with a fertile imagination!

The monument, which dates back to 2700BC, was broken into by Vikings, who left Runic inscriptions – or graffiti – on the walls, telling stories of their women back home and, intriguingly, hidden treasure.

Riding of the Marches. The Riding of the Marches around Kirkwall was reintroduced in 1986 to celebrate the 500th anniversary of the town being awarded Royal Burgh status by King James III of Scotland. It has since become a colourful annual event on the Orkney calendar in August.

The procession can comprise almost 90 horses and carriages going around the perimeter of the town, but the highlights are when they leave Broad Street, in front of St Magnus Cathedral, and at Scapa beach, when the horses have a well-earned wade though the water.

The Riding of the Marches is announced traditionally through the streets of the town and at the Merkat Cross by a halberdier (Bryan Taylor) and a drummer (Mike Stout).

Stromness Primary School. The school (roll 150) is one of the latest additions to the educational infrastructure of the islands. It was built in 2012/13 as part of a multi-million-pound development package which included four other new public buildings:

Kirkwall Grammar School (roll 820). The building (currently under construction) is of a spectacular design, and will comprise a variety of materials, including copper cladding, natural stone, and the extensive use of glass, to give what has been described as an "Orkney Feel". The building will also incorporate a circular-fronted Arts Theatre for general public use.

The School Hostel – for school pupils from the outer islands who are unable to get home on a daily basis. The hostel is also under construction (as we go to press), but it has already been acknowledged by the local council that it will not have enough accommodation!

Pickaquoy Centre extension. The centre for leisure, sport and arts is situated near to the Peerie Sea in Kirkwall and was built around the millennium. The extension, includes a swimming pool, squash courts and other sporting facilities.

In the present unforgiving economic climate, these projects could not have been timed better, and have provided employment and some stability for the local construction industry.

The county has two secondary schools, four junior high schools (off Mainland) and 17 primary schools. Some of these are under threat because of spending cutbacks and falling rolls.

Marinas. The popularity of pleasure sailing and cruising around the coast of Britain has, rather belatedly, reached Orkney within the past twenty or so years as many UK yachtsmen begin to realise there is something to see and enjoy north of the Caledonian Canal!

To be fair, the facilities for visiting boats to Orkney were so-so for a long time, but now there are three principal marinas – Kirkwall, Stromness and Westray – providing more than 170 berths, with various services. This awakening to the potential of yachting still has some way to go, but many in the sailing fraternity are catching on to the fact that Orkney not only provides good cruising, but is also a stepping stone to Shetland and Scandinavia.

Air Services. Scheduled air services in and out of Orkney are run by a subsidised franchise of Loganair and Flybe. There are connections to the main Scottish cities on a daily basis, and Loganair also operates a service from Kirkwall to the smaller islands.

Islander aircraft, like the one pictured, have operated the internal isles service with excellent reliability and, at one time, provided the air ambulance service – replaced by a Scottish Mainland-based service against the wishes of most islanders.

Islander aircraft land on grass airstrips mostly, and the flight from Westray to Papa Westray is the shortest scheduled flight in the world, officially timed at 120 seconds – although it has recently been done in 53 seconds.

PARK
G-BPCA

EYNHALLOW

NOUP HEAD, WESTRAY

John Rae. In 2013, Orkney marked the bicentennial of this Orcadian's birth. If his name is unfamiliar do not despair, because he is probably *the* unsung hero of Orkney's entire history.

John Rae is an Orcadian hero who made his name in Canada as an explorer in the 1800s. He is regarded by many as the finest Arctic pioneer but, unfortunately, he has never been given the international recognition he deserves. Quite the reverse, in fact: he was vilified by the establishment.

He is, of course, recognised in his native islands, and this powerful memorial is situated in St Magnus Cathedral.

Rae's success in surveying the land mass of northern Canada and surviving the atrocious weather conditions when doing "field work", was due , in part, to the fact that he respected the culture of the native Inuit, and adopted many of their survival skills.

The quest to find the North West Passage through the north of Canada was high on the agenda of the British authorities at the time and resulted in a number of expeditions, including the disastrous Franklin Expedition. Rae later published evidence he had received from the Inuit about the fate of Franklin, including accounts that the crew resorted to cannibalism, in a last-ditch effort to survive. These reports proved unacceptable to the British authorities, and Franklin's widow ran a highly successful (and unfair) campaign to discredit Rae.

In fact, Rae was the first to identify and map the last navigable channel of the Passage in 1854, and Roald Amundsen, who was the first to successfully navigate the entire route, described Rae's work as of "incalculable value".

The Brig o' Waithe. Many visitors to Orkney drive over this brig as part of the main Stromness to Kirkwall road and are unaware of the significance of the area.

The Brig o' Waithe is at the mouth of the Loch of Stenness, on the edge of Scapa Flow.

In March, 1940, German bombers appeared over Orkney to bomb the Royal Naval base and were engaged by British fighter aircraft. The Germans jettisoned their high explosive and incendiary bombs near to the brig and killed a local man, who was standing in the doorway of his home.

James Isbister, whose wife had just given birth to a son, was aged only 27, and became the first British civilian air raid casualty of World War Two.

Standing Stones of Stenness. A wintry scene where the Lochs of Stenness and Harray meet.

In the foreground is what is known as the Watchstone once one of a pair – and their role or significance is open to speculation.

To the rear of the picture are the Standing Stones of Stenness, which originally formed a ring of 12 and, at heights of up to 19 feet, are considerably taller than the ones at the nearby Ring of Brodgar. It is believed that the positions of the stones have lunar and solar significance.

Sadly, a number of years ago some of the stones were removed by a local farmer, including what was called the Odin Stone. This megalith had a hole through which lovers clasped hands to pledge their undying love for each other.

Dated at 3000BC, the Standing Stones of Stenness are one of the earliest stone circles in Britain.

St Magnus Cathedral. Work to build a Viking cathedral in Kirkwall, on what was then the shore of the Peerie Sea (now a boating pond as you enter Kirkwall from the west), started in 1137 on the orders of Earl Rognvald Kolsson, in memory of his uncle Earl Magnus, who was murdered on the island of Egilsay.

Both men were canonised and their remains were laid to rest in two pillars within the building.

The cathedral is owned by the people of Orkney, not by a church, and the building is managed and financed on their behalf by Orkney Islands Council. The Society for the Friends of St Magnus raises additional funds for the upkeep of the building, and there is a continuous programme of repairs (and restoration work) to the red sandstone.

Weekly Church of Scotland services are held in the building, but other Christian denominations can use the cathedral, and in recent years it has also been a spectacular venue for music and the arts.

Wartime Defences. Any visitor to Orkney cannot fail to see the remains of huge, abandoned concrete lookout posts and gun emplacements, such as this one at Breckan in Holm. It is an indication of Orkney's strategic importance during both world wars – something that cannot be overstated – and particularly that of the sheltered naval anchorage of Scapa Flow.

In fact, during the Second World War, Orkney was fortified to such an extent that, outside London, it had one of the biggest defence networks in the country. What the visitor sees is really only the tip of the iceberg, as there is much more in inaccessible and remote spots. A book has been published recently, *Orkney at War,* by Geoffrey Stell, which documents the defences in detail.

Only recently has the true archaeological and tourism value of these structures been realised, and visitors can now visit the Ness Battery in Stromness and have a guided tour.

Ness Battery. This picture at the battery shows a surveyor at work recording the details of the structure in minute detail, as it is now regarded as an archaeological site. Unfortunately, this particular store, where the ammunition was kept, is out of bounds to visitors, but the battery is well worth a visit, if only to see the mural in the canteen!

There was a battery at Ness in both world wars and it guarded the entrance to Scapa Flow from the west, but it was only part of an extensive defensive strategy which included every available contraption and device to "stop the Jerries getting in". Again, the book *Orkney at War* details these measures.

Castle of Yesnaby. Some of the most picturesque coastal scenery in Orkney can be found on the west coast of the Mainland and, arguably, the jewel in the crown is the area of Yesnaby. The cliff scenery is spectacular, and visitors can park on the site of an old wartime gun emplacement and walk a short distance (20 minutes) to the Castle of Yesnaby itself.

For the more energetic, a walk from Yesnaby, north past Skaill to Costa Head, or the opposite way, to Stromness, is very rewarding, with excellent scenery and numerous sea stacks, the pick of which is North Gaulton Castle. These walks (for some inexplicable reason) are not guided in any way.

Whisky. Only teetotallers come to Orkney and leave again without sampling the county's whisky. The best known is Highland Park, which is branded and marketed around the world, but there is also a lesser-known Orcadian dram, called Scapa.

Highland Park Distillery is situated just outside Kirkwall and is open to visitors. It dates back to 1798, but the origin of the whisky probably dates back to a man called Magnus Eunson, whose bothy was on this site.

According to W. R. Mackintosh, in the book *Around the Orkney Peat-Fires,* Magnus 'Mansie' Eunson was "a flesher [butcher], beadle, and a successful smuggler. In addition to this he was a born character, brimful of pawky humour and resource, which extricated him from many a scrape."

Scapa Distillery, just across Scapa Bay from Highland Park, is not in active production, but the whisky is still available in shops.

Beer and wine. Orkney adequately caters for whisky drinkers, but those who prefer beer are not forgotten, and the islands have two breweries, both located in the West Mainland.

The Orkney Brewery (which has a visitor centre) kicked into production in 1988, and has received a number of awards for its range of beers, which includes the intriguingly named *Skull Splitter*. It has a volume of 8.5 % so, for those who may over-imbibe, the warning is in the name!

The other Orkney beers come from the Swannay-based brewery of Rob Hill, which also has a heavyweight in the form of *Orkney Porter*, which weighs in at a hefty 9%!

However, the personal favourite of this writer – and one that it is very highly recommended – is Scapa Special, particularly on draught. Not all local pubs stock it, but they should!

P.S. Orkney's alcoholic beverage range also includes Orkney Wine, based near the Italian Chapel, which celebrated its tenth birthday in 2013.

TIMELINE
SCOTTISH RULE IN ORKNEY
1878
SCHOOLHOUSE, QUOYLOO

Italian Chapel. The Italian Chapel is on the island of Lamb holm and is known throughout the world.

After Churchill ordered the defences of Scapa Flow to be reinforced in 1939 and the building of inter-island barriers, 550 Italian prisoners of war were shipped to Orkney from North Africa to provide much-needed labour. It was illegal for prisoners to be deployed on military-related work so, rather neatly for the British, they were used in the construction of *causeways.*

The POWs appealed for the provision of a chapel in which to worship and, once permission was granted by their captors, set about converting a metal Nissen hut. The prisoners, and a man named Domenico Chiocchetti in particular, salvaged what materials they could from around Camp 60 and slowly, but surely, realised their dream.

The result is what we see today: a beautiful, ornate and moving symbol of war, peace and reconciliation.

Orkney Chairs. Traditional straw-backed Orkney chairs go back centuries in the islands. At one time, they were a practical necessity for poor crofters and ubiquitous because the straw was cheap and easily obtainable.

Nowadays, they are viewed in a completely different light – as luxury, up-market items of furniture – and are in demand all around the world. The one pictured is of a familiar design, but they come in all shapes and sizes, with hoods, mini ones for children, and matching stools.

There are several craftsmen on the islands who make them, and pictured is Kevin Gauld ("The Orkney Furniture Maker") who, with his uncle, actually grows the oats to to create the straw backs. He also makes high-quality bespoke furniture such as tables and cabinets.

Old, antique Orkney chairs fetch good prices at furniture auctions in central Scotland.

ROUSAY

SNOW ON THE HOY HILLS

Kirkwall. The cathedral still dominates the Kirkwall skyline despite modern architecture and the general development of the town. Over the years there has been a general depopulation of the country areas in favour of urban living, presumably partly for social reasons, and the bigger events and amenities tend to be in the towns, and particularly Kirkwall.

In the picture, to the right of the cathedral, is the hideously designed school hostel for isles pupils. It is scheduled for demolition, to be replaced by a marginally more attractive building.

Ness of Brodgar. Until 2002, this area was nothing more than a thin strip of land separating the Harray and Stenness lochs, best known for being the site of the Ring of Brodgar.

But that has all changed. Over the past few years, excavations have revealed a huge complex of "monumental" Stone Age buildings, the like of which surprised even the archaeologists.

In 2008, five years after the first tantalizing glimpse of a Neolithic building on the Ness, the excavators uncovered "one of the largest, if not *the* largest, stone-built Neolithic non-funerary structures in Britain."

Going by the name of Structure Ten, the building is one of a number of large, elaborate buildings on the Ness. Although earlier geophysics scans suggested there was something very large under the turf, it took excavation to reveal the sheer scale of what lay beneath. Measuring 25 metres (82 feet) long by 20 metres (65 feet) wide, the five-metre-thick outer walls remain to a height of approximately one metre (three feet).

In 2011, radiocarbon dates from two areas of the site showed that the prehistoric complex on the Ness was in use for around 1,000 years — from at least 3200BC to around 2300BC.

A computer generated artist's impression of the Ness.

Agriculture. Orkney has a fairly diverse economy but – aside from the Flotta oil terminal development – the lynchpins of the local economy are farming and tourism.

By sheer hard work, and careful marketing, the islands have developed an enviable reputation for producing quality food, including prime beef, lamb, shellfish and even locally made ice cream and fudge.

There is excellent pasture and soil for agriculture, but unpredictable and inclement weather can make farming a hazardous business. Over the centuries, resourceful Orcadians have tilled the land to feed their families, and nowadays there is an active food and livestock export business. However, a recent economic blow was the closure of Orkney Meat, an island-based meat-processing company, and Orkney Herring.

The showcase for farming in Orkney is in August, when there are a number of agricultural shows, culminating in the County Show, where this fine specimen won his rosettes. Thousands of people flock to Kirkwall for the show, and the weekend on which it falls is the highlight of the Orkney calendar, with many other events at that time also.

324

The Ba'. Our three pictures show the beginning and an end to the Kirkwall Ba' (ball) game.

On Christmas and New Year's Days the narrow streets of Kirkwall are jam-packed with players and spectators for the Ba'.

This is an ancient street ball game, but with no rules other than the two sides – the Uppies and Doonies – have to touch a cork-filled leather ball at a goal, at either end of the town, in order to win the contest. The game is *extremely* physical and not for the faint-hearted!

Four games are played during the festive period, two each for men and boys, and generate huge excitement among a vocal crowd of supporters.

The men's game usually lasts several hours and, once the game has been settled, the winning side has an internecine debate to "elect" a winner, who is allowed to keep the ba'.

Our pictures show the throw up of a men's ba' at the Merkat Cross, in front of St Magnus Cathedral. The other two show the dramatic conclusion of a boys' game and a Doonie victory, when they throw the ball into the sea (and subsequently retrieve it, of course!). Spectators often do not actually witness the moment the ba' hits the water, so our photographer, Tom O'Brien, deserves top marks!

OWEN
7

HMS *Royal Oak*. The battleship was sunk while at anchor in the supposedly safe harbour of Scapa Flow in 1939 – not long after the outbreak of war – by a German U-boat, before the Churchill Barriers were built. Eight hundred and thirty three sailors lost their lives in the disaster, which shocked the naval authorities in Whitehall.

The hulk of the vessel is a war grave and marked by a beacon. Each year, on the anniversary of the sinking, a short service is conducted over her and wreaths are "laid" on the water. Three participants of the service are pictured: Malcolm Johnston of the Royal British Legion, bugler Billy Stanger, and piper Mike Parkins.

www.nlb.org.uk

Barriers and Blockships. The Churchill Barriers (or causeways) link four islands to the Orkney Mainland, and were built during the Second World War to safeguard the naval anchorage of Scapa Flow for the British Fleet.

The order to build them was triggered by the sinking of the battleship *Royal Oak* at her mooring in Scapa Flow, in 1939, by a German U-boat. The daring German submarine commander, Gunther Prien, slipped past the inadequate British defences and through the Kirk Sound channel (between Holm and Lamb holm) under cover of darkness. His torpedo attack on the *Oak* was decisive, and he slipped back out of the "safe" naval anchorage using the same route by which he had entered.

A stunned Churchill and Admiralty subsequently ordered the construction of the barriers, made from huge concrete blocks, to seal off entrances to Scapa Flow. These entrances had previously been protected by sunken blockships, the remains of which can still be seen today alongside the barriers.

These blockships should not be confused with the wrecks of the entire German High Seas Fleet, which was dramatically scuttled in Scapa Flow after the end of World War One.

THE CHURCHILL BARRIERS

Festival of the Horse and Boys' Ploughing Match. This is an annual event in South Ronaldsay in August. The girls dress up in highly ornate costumes to play the role of "horses", while the boys compete in a ploughing match, using miniature ploughs, on the beach of the Sands o' Wright. It is an interesting and colourful spectacle, but watch out for the intensity among dads and grandfathers spectating the ploughing!

STENNESS

A STORMY DAY IN ORKNEY

Weather. It is perhaps not surprising that weather is an almost constant topic of conversation among Orcadians, given the islands' geographical position. It has the same latitude as St Petersburg in Russia but, thanks to the Gulf Steam, the winters are not so harsh! Nevertheless, winters can be long, dark and stormy. On the other hand, the summers enjoy long daylight hours and there are even midnight golf competitions!

For the purposes of this book, however, we concentrate on the more dramatic, stormy winter, with two pictures of the Churchill Barriers where, despite the warning sign, police are needed to deter motorists "going for it!". A number of years ago a "wave wall" was constructed at the side of Barrier Number Two in an effort to make crossings safer in rough weather, but public opinion of its effectiveness is fairly negative. Some actually think it is now *more* dangerous.

The third picture is of the m.v. *Hamnavoe,* the daily ferry from Stromness to the Scottish mainland, ploughing through heavy seas in Hoy Sound.

NO STOPPING
ON CAUSEWAY
DRIVERS CROSS
AT OWN RISK
POLICE
Scotland
CRIMESTOPPERS
0800 555 111
www.northern.police.uk
Northern
Constabulary
POLICE

Tomb of the Eagles. The name itself triggers the imagination, and the entrance to this chambered cairn – by trolley – makes this particularly attractive to younger visitors! There is also a visitor centre, where some of the artefacts from the excavation can be handled.

Dating back to Neolithic times, the cairn was expertly excavated by a local farmer, the late Ronnie Simison, whose family now run the facility.

The tomb gets its name from the sea eagle bones that were found alongside the remains of over 300 humans. The eagles probably had some symbolic power and the human bones were weathered, indicating that they had been exposed to the elements before being buried.

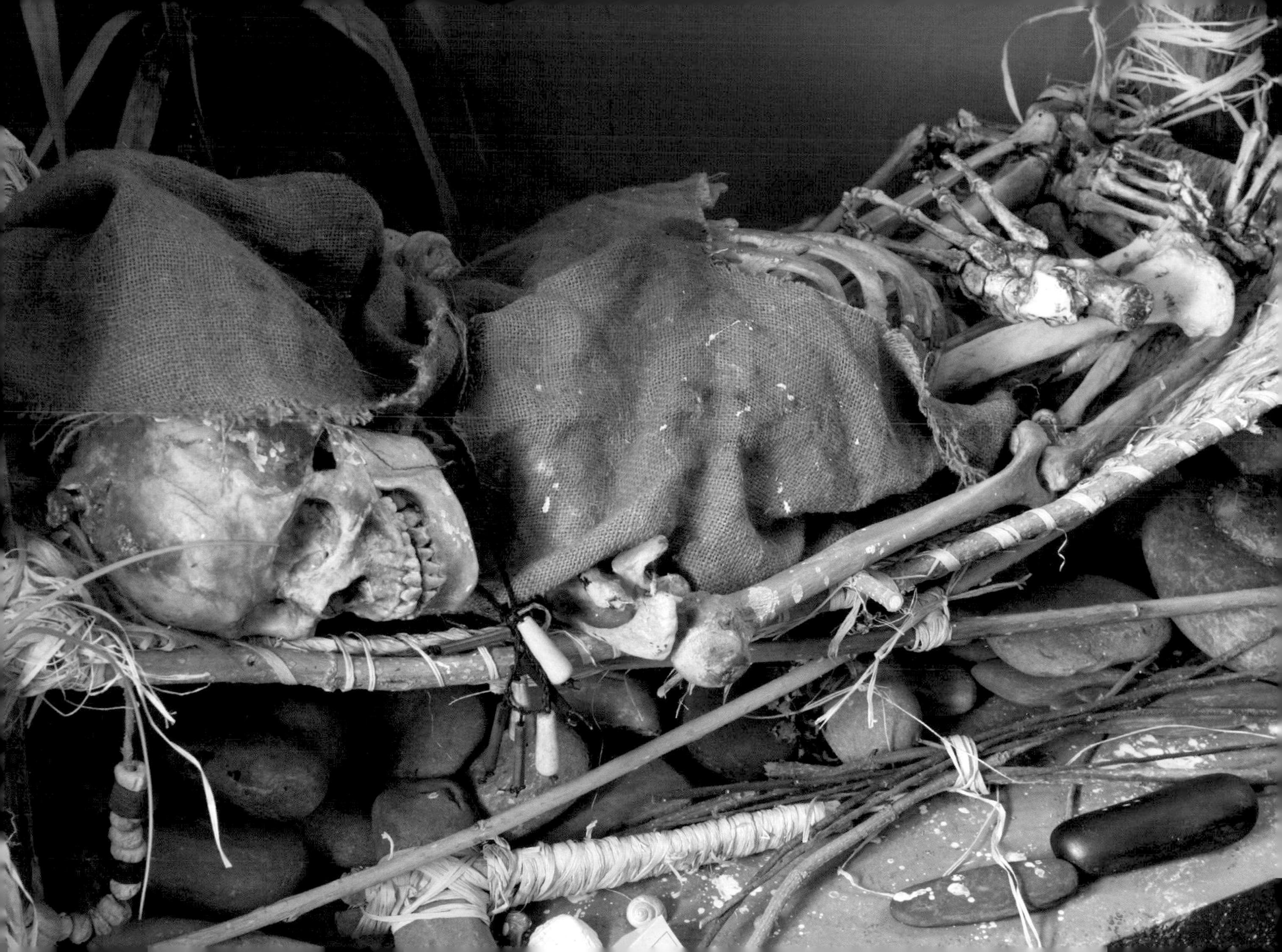

Stromness. This is the smaller of Orkney's two towns and is the arrival port for the islands' principal ferry link with the Scottish mainland.

Nestled under Ward Hill, or Brinkie's Brae, it offers a picturesque welcome to ferry passengers arriving from Scrabster, with its little private quays all along the seafront. Once ashore, the cobbled streets and quaint narrow lanes give Stromness a special charm and character.

Hamnavoe (haven bay) as it was once known, developed as a port in the 1660s, supplying passing ships en route around Britain or heading west to Canada, to open new frontiers. Ships from the Hudson's Bay Company called at Stromness extensively and, by 1817, the town had 38 ale houses to quench the thirst of parched seamen.

Stromness was home to two of Orkney's famous sons, the writer and poet, George Mackay Brown, who died in 1996, and the painter, Stanley Curister. The latter was limner to the Queen and made his home on the edge of town in the twilight of his life.

Earl's Palace. What remains of the impressive Earl's Palace lies in the centre of Kirkwall, alongside St Magnus Cathedral and the Bishop's Palace, with its distinctive "Moosie Toor" (mouse tower).

It was built in the early 1600s by the infamous Earl Patrick Stewart and has many fine features, including a Great Hall.

Patrick Stewart was a hated earl of Orkney who had a reputation for greed and extravagance. He maltreated local people, but came unstuck when he ran into financial difficulties. He was subsequently charged with treason and incarcerated in Edinburgh Castle. Five years later "Black Patie", as he was known, was executed, aged 40.

His palace passed through various hands during the next century but, despite its splendour, it was unoccupied and uninhabitable by the early 1700s and fifty years later the roof was removed.

Like many of Orkney's historic sites, it is sometimes used as a venue during local festivals.

Marwick Head, Birsay. On the evening of June 5, 1916 HMS Hampshire was sunk off Marwick Head with an appalling loss of life, including Lord Kitchener, the Minister for War. The vessel was en route to Russia in extremely heavy seas when she struck a German mine. Almost 650 people lost their lives.

The sinking was shrouded in mystery and various theories were floated about the circumstances of the disaster, including sabotage, but none were proved.

There was, however, huge unhappiness among Orcadians about how the authorities handled the rescue attempt. The lifeboat at Stromness was not launched and local people were prevented from going to the coastline to search for and help possible survivors.

The Kitchener's Memorial on Marwick Head was unveiled in 1926 after a fund raising campaign by the Orkney community.

Festivals. Over the past 40 years, a number of festivals have been established, and Orkney hosts an event nearly every month during the summer. They include festivals of folk music, jazz, blues and science, attracting well-known international names. Dolly Parton is pictured.

Probably the best-known event is the St Magnus Festival and Magfest, which is devoted to the arts and mainly orchestral music. It was started in 1977 by a group led by Sir Peter Maxwell Davies, and has grown into one of Britain's "most highly regarded and adventurous arts events". Sir Peter lives in Orkney and is Master of the Queen's Music.

P.S. Nearly fooled you! Our 'Dolly Parton' was a tribute act whose trip to Orkney was nearly a disaster. After "Dolly" arrived in Orkney she realised her "hair" had been left behind, and an aircraft was flown south specially to retrieve it. It got to Orkney in the nick of time!

ERRY
INN
Gibson

Skara Brae. The ancient village of Skara Brae, in the parish of Sandwick, is older than the Pyramids of Egypt, and is one of the most outstanding monuments in the world.

The Neolithic village, a tight group of dwelling houses, lies on the edge of Skaill Bay and was first uncovered after a storm in 1850. The structures had been preserved in sand and, when meaningful excavations were made in the late 1920s, the magnitude and importance of the discovery was realised.

Modern dating methods now estimate that the village dates back to 3200BC – 2200BC.

An interpretation centre is near to the site, including an "as it was" replica, so visitors can get a real feel for life in the Stone Age.

SKARA BRAE

Westray Wife. Her posh title is Orkney Venus, but she is known in Orkney as the "Westray Wife" and is the earliest representation of a human figure to be found in Scotland.

This rare find was unearthed during an archaeological excavation in Westray in 2009 and, apart from the obvious human shape, there are scratches and abrasions for a nose, mouth, hair and breasts. Two small indentations represent eyes.

ORKNEY'S
US?

Sport. The sports pages of the island newspaper *The Orcadian* are packed every week with reports and pictures covering a wide range of activities, the popular ones being football, rugby, hockey and netball. In order to be competitive, Orkney teams travel south on a regular basis to play, and often young people devote their entire weekend to just travelling to and from the matches, such is their dedication.

Pictured is action from a hotly contested Parish Cup Final. The final is always played on County Show night in Kirkwall and is the highlight of the football season. The competition itself has unique rules, with strict conditions on eligibility depending on birthplace and residence. The towns are excluded, and any parish boundary changes are fiercely debated and challenged!

The Parish Cup matches – together with Orkney Rugby Club games – usually attract good partisan crowds who keep themselves well refreshed!

JAKO
B & L
BUILDERS

Renewable Energy. Orkney is at the world forefront of research and development into renewable energy. The publically funded European Marine Energy Centre (EMEC) is based in the islands and is the first of its kind in the world, providing purpose-built open-sea testing facilities for companies interested in developing energy-generating machines from tide and wave power.

EMEC has 14 full-scale berths for test devices, such as the "Oyster" pictured, and two scale test sites. The attraction of Orkney and EMEC to developers, from as far away as Japan, is that extremely harsh sea conditions are on the islands' 'doorstep', coupled with very sheltered seascapes and numerous harbours offering various ancillary services. £30m in public cash has been ploughed into EMEC, and in 2011 it announced it was "financially self-sufficient" due to increased commercial activity the previous year. Much of the testing is conducted at Billia Croo, near Stromness.

The Oyster is being developed by a company called Aquamarine Power and is designed for inshore waters. A wave-powered pump, it pushes high-pressure water ashore to drive a land-based hydro-electric turbine.

STROMNESS

WESTRAY

Wind turbines. The development of renewable energy is seen as an up-and-coming industry for the future in Orkney and may cushion the decline of North Sea oil-related income. However, many warn that it should not be at "any cost", and the proliferation of wind turbines, in particular, is a cause for concern among many local people, who think they are a blight on the landscape and damage tourism. This is likely to be an on-going debate, with local planning policies at the centre of it.

Ring of Brodgar. The Ring of Brodgar, part of the Heart of Neolithic Orkney World Heritage Site, is one of the islands' most impressive monuments.

The ring – or henge – of upright stones forms a perfect circle, with a diameter of 340 feet, the stones themselves varying from seven to 15 feet in height.

There were originally 60 standing stones but only 27 now remain.

The ring is thought to date back to 2500 – 2000BC, and the positions of the stones are reckoned to have astronomical significance.

A short walk from the ring is the Ness of Brodgar – and its temple-like structures – then, a little further on, are the Standing Stones of Stenness. Exciting finds at the Ness excavations each year – by the Orkney Research Centre for Archaeology – fuel speculation about the relationship that used to exist between these three sites.

Puffins. Puffins, with their highly-coloured and distinctive beaks, are a hugely popular attraction for visitors to Orkney.

Tim Dean, in his excellent *The Orkney Book of Birds*, writes "apart from their colourful and patterned clown-faces that present an expression of sadness, doom and depression, they usually allow the visitor a confiding intimacy that most other birds do not.

"They are primarily burrowers but can also be found tenanting holes and crevices in cliff faces."

They can be observed on many Mainland locations, but they prefer offshore islands, and Orkney's largest colony is on uninhabited Sule Skerry, where there are 60,000 occupied burrows.

A comprehensive and colourful guide to the islands' birdlife can be found in Tim Dean's book.

YESNABY

PIEROWALL, WESTRAY

North Ronaldsay. The most northerly island in the Orkney archipelago, North Ronaldsay, is home to a rare breed of sheep.

North Ronaldsay sheep are unique. They are retained on the beach by a drystane dyke that goes around the entire island, and live on seaweed, except in the spring, when ewes and lambs are allowed on grassland for three or four months.

The diet of the small sheep gives their meat a very distinctive flavour.

Old Man of Hoy. Orkney's oldest inhabitant is situated on the west coast of the island, and visitors arriving on a Stromness-bound ferry get an early introduction to him en route.

Hoy is Norse for High Island and it is easy to see why.

The Old Man is the tallest sea stack in Britain at 449 feet (137m) and, although it was only first climbed in 1966, by a team which included Chris Bonington, it is now scaled on a regular basis.

The path to the Old Man starts at Rackwick Bay and is almost four miles long, over fairly rough moorland. Walkers will also, in all probability, be "dive bombed" by great skuas, or "bonxies"!

Rackwick Bay. For many Orcadians, Orkney's finest spot is Rackwick Bay in Hoy – a magnificent, sweeping, boulder-strewn bay, with towering red sandstone cliffs, several miles from the Old Man of Hoy.

The area can be reached by car but, for many, the magic of Rackwick can only be fully appreciated after taking the short ferry ride from Stromness to Moaness and then trekking through the valley in the shadow of Ward Hill.

Index